TUMBLEWEEDS

TUMBLEWEEDS

AJ ANGLEBERGER

Pine Bird Press

Copyright © 2024 by AJ Angleberger

All rights reserved. No part of this book may be reproduced in any manner whatsoever without written permission except in the case of brief quotations embodied in critical articles and reviews.

ISBN: 979-8-9909510-0-6

First Printing, 2024

Dedicated to my grandfather,
who loved reading poetry and lived
vicariously through my postcards.

And for every wild soul
that feels at home on the open road.

Contents

Dedication — v

my sweet escape — 1

dissociation — 2

waiting for you — 3

travel companion — 4

the freeway is calling, and I must go — 5

see you later — 6

naturally — 7

central time — 8

fortune cookie oyster shell — 9

infinity — 10

wallow — 11

mental snapshot — 12

libra scales — 13

liminal spaces — 14

atlas	15
sunset in the canyon	16
inner peace	17
okay, I'm ready	18
haiku 1	19
out of sight, out of mind	20
a magician never reveals her secrets	21
6pm	22
long distance relationships	23
solar power	24
rescue breaths	25
turning 26	26
match the frequency	27
ocean city, maryland	28
epitaph	29
nine to five	30
at dusk	31
the little things	32
aggregation	33
moths to the flame	34
goodbyes from country skies	35

catching up in my journal — 36

tumbleweed — 37

spence hot springs — 38

natural beauty — 39

one way ticket — 40

hot child in the city — 41

move — 42

full moon before yule — 43

honeymoon suite — 44

no echoes — 45

compassion — 46

sanctuary — 47

omaha, nebraska — 48

growth is messy — 49

one on one — 50

rose tinted shot glass — 51

perspective — 52

elevated emotions — 53

vision board — 54

sanguine — 55

the fire within — 56

headed to forever 57

siren song 58

home 59

expansion 60

the vagabond 61

pause 62

wisconsin 63

blue hole, new mexico 64

opportunities 65

staying the night in arkansas 66

farewell 67

About The Author 68

my sweet escape

I'd like to get lost
In an abandoned mansion
In the woods at sunrise
In a crowd of bustling strangers
In between the pages
of your anatomy textbook
In the eyes of a modest soul
with otherworldly ideas
I'd like to wander
Itinerary abstract
A topographic map under my feet
Golden compass sun in the east
I don't want to be found today

dissociation

I want to get away from it all
And by it all
I mean myself

waiting for you

Don't be afraid of leaving home
The universe is your living room

My desert flower
Only the brave
Will see the bloom

I guarantee you it's possible
To leave your hometown
That your dreams still come in color
2,000 miles from your mother

Baby
They have coffee shops
And grocery stores in California, too
Waiting for you

travel companion

Get in my suitcase
You're all I need

the freeway is calling, and I must go

I miss someone that I've never met
I crave a place that doesn't exist
FOMO has entered the chat

I need tuna packet dinners
Parking lot sunrises
Scenery rushing by the window
Singing to a dusty dashboard
With my best friend

No plans
No destinations
No sense of time

see you later

It may feel like I'm gone
But I promise
I'm somewhere missing you

naturally

Expectations are a buzzkill
Let life surprise you
Embrace the detours
Bliss awaits

central time

Let's cross a border
I wanna lose an hour with you

fortune cookie oyster shell

When I opened my clenched fist there were four tiny crescent moons in my palm. I watched them slowly fill with shiny sweat. A summer rain kisses the roof. The water stain on the ceiling... It's shaped like a seahorse. Don't you think? We took it as a sign to drive to the beach. The trees in the distance seemed to be giving us a standing ovation. We arrive to sandy carpets at our budget motel. The Sunoco gas station sign looks like a full moon rising. It could be just as pretty, if you don't think about it. The waves wash away our confessions, written in the sand. Kiss me in the lifeguard chair. Sway with me in the shallows. Spin me around this low tide dance floor.

infinity

Sand in my teeth
Salt in my eyes
My sinuses burn
Summer crowds
Umbrella army
In a row
Like a defensive line
The endless horizon
Water and sky
I thought green was open
Blue has never felt so free

wallow

Be like a sponge
Soak it all in
The good with the bad
You'll wring yourself out later

mental snapshot

I closed my eyes
And opened my heart
To breathe in this moment

Etching this feeling
      onto paper
      onto celluloid
      onto my soul

I'm capturing this memory
      to cling to in fits of anxiety
      to savor on my deathbed
      to revisit in my dreams

libra scales

I don't know what's worse
Feeling like the world is too small
Will I see it all and become jaded?

Or that it's too big
And I'll never cover enough distance
In my insignificance

liminal spaces

Can I stay here?
In this moment
Between day and night
Between you and me
In the space between
the driver and passenger seat
Can I stay here forever, please?

atlas

I don't want the places I wander
To live only in photographs
Let's pull over
Get to know the land with our feet

I'm making maps with my body
Tracing the borders
With a long-legged pace
Walking the intricacies of stone and sand
Memorizing landscapes with bare soles

Imploring earth
Imprint your stories
On my bare soul

sunset in the canyon

I thought if I saw
Something beautiful
I wouldn't be so sad
And in this moment
I was right

inner peace

I had filled my life up
With so much noise and chaos
That I had forgotten
The comfort silence holds for me
I'm listening now

okay, I'm ready

Hey wild love
Grow on me for a while
Explore me like an atlas
Wander with me
Through the woods
Through life
You're good at getting lost
I'm good at finding the way home
I know I said I was scared
But I've been thinking
About you and I
About liquid skies
About chasing sunrise
With you

haiku 1

To plug in, to fully charge
You have to lie still
In the green, dirty outdoors

out of sight, out of mind

In the flowing fog
We lost ourselves
I turned around
And you were gone

Walking to the tree line
My breath the only sound
The damp grass licks my shins

Monocacy River sits still
Like a scolded child
White mist floats atop
Flowing through the young forest

In the silence of this moment
I've never felt more alone

a magician never reveals her secrets

Why does it only dew
when you're not looking?
You run inside to grab a sweater
and the world is soaked upon your return

6pm

Sunsets are dependable and fickle all at once
The forest snares the day, tree by tree
A small fire somewhere is started again

long distance relationships

We talk about you behind your back
The moon and I
I climb onto the roof
And we converse through the night
In whispers, so as not to wake you
I tell her about the love
blooming in my stomach
She listens to my heart purr
And she wishes she could feel it too
Puzzled, I reassure her,
"But everybody loves you,
You're the moon!"

solar power

Love affair
With the morning sun
Golden as the honey runs
Awaiting kisses
At the break of dawn
Shine on me
Til darkness comes

rescue breaths

She had blue eyes
Of course
But not the kind of blue
That you could drown in
It was more of the blue sky
That saves you from drowning
When you can't figure out
Which way is up

turning 26

Breathless and dripping with sea water. Wringing out my short hair; droplets on my tan skin. I feel raw, feminine, alive. The ocean pulled me in as a child and I emerged from the waves a woman. A daughter of Amphitrite; reborn from her tidal womb. With hips and tits and wild hair. Salt scrubbed clean. Gifted the ocean's power: her constant rhythm. My freckled skin hugs my new curves. My eyes are shining brighter, containing a raging starburst inside: the summer sun. My youth dances just beneath my flesh. Pounding from inside. Screaming, "Let's go!"

match the frequency

Crowds are like the ocean

You can tire yourself out
fighting the waves

Or a simple dead man's float
can take you back to shore

ocean city, maryland

Not even halfway back to the motel
Our feet were dead
We walked off the glaring boardwalk
And onto the darkened beach
The waves kissed our tired toes
The sand caressed our soles
The ocean was black
Except for the thin white lines
That would appear in the distance
And grow larger as they approach
Curling into bubbling waves on the coast
Meteors shoot across the sky
Bouncing off the ebony sea
They followed us all the way back
To the Thunderbird Motel
Sand in the bedsheets
In the shower
In my soul

epitaph

Morning light
Too bright
Sore legs
Bruises with unknown origins
Texts with unknown recipients
And my shoes in my purse

It was all a blur
But the pictures are in focus

nine to five

It hits me
The taste of your tongue

We're miles apart
But you're right next to me

Living under my skin

at dusk

The sky fades into purple
As the earth turns away from the sun
Tall sunflowers sway in the breeze
Humidity hangs in the black tree line
Mellow voices on the porch
We count lamplit houses in the distance

the little things

How can you sulk among such beauty?
Melancholia at the riverbank
Why don't you flow like the stream beside you?
Let your concerns slide downstream
Sway with the cattails
Shimmer in the sun
Just be
It's that easy

aggregation

Don't follow me
It takes a shield of humor
And calloused feet
I used to complain of the rocks in my path
I had to learn that's what keeps it all in place
A rootless path would simply erode into the sea

moths to the flame

Social butterflies
would starve
without wallflowers

goodbyes from country skies

The sky is divided, perfectly in half. A straight line from horizon to horizon. On one side a massive cloud of dense white overcast. And on the other a vast, black night sky; dotted with distant suns. It's cold tonight, nearly freezing. But sight is the only sense that's fully registering the elements. I lay down to take it all in. An expansive and brilliant view. The clouds race forward to reveal a waning moon. Slowly my other senses return. First I hear silence. Then I feel cold.

catching up in my journal

Epiphanies
sandwiched between
Catastrophes

tumbleweed

I am constantly changing...evolving
Shedding skins like a snake
Every step onto new land
I gain another puzzle piece

Each miscalculation and wrong turn
Has led me to unexpected beauties
The days that end with blistered feet
Are the best days of my life

I'm finding myself
     in traffic jams
     sketchy motels
     and rest stop bathrooms
Each crossing through uncharted waters
I am becoming whole

I climbed to the top of my comfort zone
And found myself
How long have I been waiting there?

spence hot springs

I was baptized today
In a cliffside hot spring
Deep in the warm womb of the earth
Purified in the Jemez Mountains

The cold, muddy uphill climb
Was all melted away
In a glittering cave

Such an easy float
Back down to earth
On freshly born wings

I was baptized today
By Mother Nature herself

natural beauty

My stomach is soft
Like a mushroom cap
My thighs ripple when I walk
Like stones skipping across a lake
My hips dance like a field of barley
In the June breeze
My breasts full like the honey moon

I am as lovely as the springtime
Springtime is just as lovely as me

one way ticket

I find myself
Backing up a few stations
In my train of thoughts
Whenever they stop for you

hot child in the city

She leaves her bed unmade
Because she thinks it looks sexy
The heat of the pavement
Rises up to her 9th story apartment
She's taking solace in the bit of shade on the balcony
Thinking about gravitational acceleration
Carelessly flicking ashes down onto the street

Bolder than casino carpets
She displays herself
Like a pie cooling on a windowsill
Warm and begging to be stolen
For anyone to take a bite

move

Are you mad
That you are not as permanent as stone?
The time you spend staring
At the mountains in envy
You too are shifting
Chipping away

full moon before yule

Breathe in the moon's energy
Notice her everlasting aura
Feel her eternal grace
See how she glows so brightly?
She hasn't dimmed with age
Be like the moon
Reflect light
Illuminate the darkness around you

honeymoon suite

It's checkout time
At heartbreak motel
Vacant sign on blink
Buzzing neon letters
Room for one more
She's patiently waiting
Dusting her frame
Wiping cobwebs
From almond eyes
Ripped out the worn pages
From the log book
Fresh paint
Clean sheets
Listening
For that bell to ring

no echoes

A lone wolf
That's how I see you
Howling to a distant moon
Sitting a spell
With the only one
Lonelier than you

compassion

For a moment
I see it
I see what you see
And I love me too

sanctuary

I want to look down
Into a forest of you
Wander your pine groves
Sip from your stream of consciousness
I'm gonna camp out
Under your stars tonight
Surrounded by everything you

omaha, nebraska

Maybe we'll move to the city
A little apartment in the sky
We could be one of those lights
Another high-rise twinkle in the night
Holding hands in traffic jams
A bodega picnic in the park
Sweet sirens sing us to sleep
Never alone, never dark

growth is messy

I want you to feel scared
I want you to feel alone
These are the moments
That you'll find yourself
      Raw and nude
You'll see where you need to catch up with your kite
I'll be there
You can crawl on my rocks
Slumber in my moss
Get lost in cavernous conversations
And come out whole on the other side
Whole, but hungry
The world has plenty of fruit to offer
Suck the nectar
Swallow the seeds

one on one

I have the time to talk
More importantly,
the time to listen
I'll look into your worried eyes
I won't quicken my pace
In search of a louder distraction
I won't shuffle my feet
To withdraw from shared intimacy
Let me read your palms like a story
Everyone has one

rose tinted shot glass

I have never met an ugly person
Never heard a sin that couldn't be forgiven
My faith in humanity is strengthened daily
My glass is perpetually half full
And I'm drinking like a fish

perspective

The trick is
To stay the pillar
And let the chaos
Happen around you
Not to you
Then you'll be able to stand back
And witness the beauty

elevated emotions

I can't avoid Colorado
Just because it makes me think of you
I have to go back
To make happier memories
To make amends

vision board

Turn your envious eyes inward
Take a piece of everything you love
And paste it together into a collage
Of the person you will become

sanguine

Do you ever feel limitless?
Like anything is possible?
And you're just thrilled to be alive?
Hold onto it for me
I'll meet you there

the fire within

A bucket list isn't for the future
It's something you live daily
May I always have boxes unchecked
A few left on the to-do's
    Things to look forward to

I hope to die with passion
I hope to die with longing
I hope to die curious
I hope to die content
    But never satisfied

headed to forever

Come here
Stand here with me
Look how far we've come
Our hearts as open
As the road we travel

siren song

The sleepy sun crept into the sky
After his underwater dive
Exploring the sea through the night
Endless waves slide to shore
Our sun glazes the ocean
With a thick, golden line
The beam of a distant flashlight
Lighthouse sun
Guide me home

home

This doesn't feel like home anymore
I only feel at home in a moving car
Listening to a distant voice over an acoustic guitar
Watching landscapes change from green to orange

I'm home on the wind
In eastern shore sunrises
And midwest sunsets
I am home in my bones
In my sunburnt skin

Home is the space between destinations
The ecotone where mountain meets meadow
Home is driving into the setting sun
The steady stars outside my window

expansion

My heart is scattered across this country
I hid a piece in a sandstone slot canyon
A sliver atop a white capped peak
Fragments sunk to the bottom of the gulf
Like anchors in the reef
I am boundless
As the wind that pushes over mountain passes
Sweeping across open valleys
Kissing wildflower prairies as she goes

the vagabond

My only constant
The only steady object in my life
Was the moon
I'm a runaway train
I'm a rolling stone
I did my makeup on the plane
Refreshing last nights mascara
Cried into clumps in a somber drunk
I don't speak in certainties
I live everywhere
Except reality
I should've answered that payphone in Missouri
It could've been you
Wait...
What state are we in?

pause

Time keeps on slipping
Sliding through my fingers
The minute hand shakes in mine
Pressing ever forward
I'm not asking for much
I don't want to go back
I just want to stay here
Just a little longer

wisconsin

Three months is enough time
To make mistakes
Enough to hide my face
I'll move on
Start over at the next place
First impressions tend to fade

blue hole, new mexico

Who I was
Before I jumped in
Was a very different person
Then I am now
Three seconds
Changed everything

opportunities

I find myself laughing
In circumstances that have had me in tears in the past
I've learned that things don't happen to me
They happen for me
    to learn
    to grow
    to become

staying the night in arkansas

I felt the humidity return in Oklahoma
Something about the thick air
Has awoken a sense of nostalgia

Feels like
    home
    summer
    fireflies

I breathe it in deeply
Like finely crushed Valium
The window stays open tonight

farewell

When you live somewhere
You can never really leave
I will haunt this place forever
Months of memories
Cries of joy and pain
Encapsulated in the walls
Sunken into the earth
My laugh echoes in these hallways
Part of me is forever here
Though I cannot stay

AJ is a creative from Frederick, Maryland, USA. Travel is her passion and latest muse. She has been living nomadically with her wife since 2018; soaking in all the inspiration her home country has to offer. Her work has previously appeared in "Orion Magazine", "Aofie's Kiss", "Thick with Conviction", and elsewhere.

Milton Keynes UK
Ingram Content Group UK Ltd.
UKHW030820010824
446082UK00003B/64